LEARN ABOUT SNOWSTORMS

By Golriz Golkar

Published by The Child's World®
1980 Lookout Drive • Mankato, MN 56003-1705
800-599-READ • www.childsworld.com

Design Elements: Shutterstock Images
Photographs ©: iStockphoto, cover (snow), 1 (snow), 6; Shutterstock Images, cover (jar), 1 (jar), 4 (paint), 10, 15, 17, 18, 21, 23; Africa Studio/Shutterstock Images, 4 (baby oil); Elizabeth A. Cummings/Shutterstock Images, 4 (food coloring); Rick Orndorf, 5; Andrew F. Kazmierski/Shutterstock Images, 9; Dmitriy Kochergin/Shutterstock Images, 13

Copyright © 2020 by The Child's World®
All rights reserved. No part of this book may be reproduced or utilized in any form or by any means without written permission from the publisher.

ISBN 9781503832145
LCCN 2018962835

Printed in the United States of America
PA02420

About the Author
Golriz Golkar is a teacher and children's author who lives in Nice, France. She enjoys cooking, traveling, and looking for ladybugs on nature walks.

TABLE OF CONTENTS

CHAPTER 1
Let's Make a Snowstorm! . . . 4

CHAPTER 2
What Causes a Snowstorm? . . . 8

CHAPTER 3
What Kinds of Snowstorms Are There? . . . 12

CHAPTER 4
Where Do Snowstorms Happen? . . . 16

Glossary . . . 22
To Learn More . . . 23
Index . . . 24

CHAPTER 1

Let's Make a Snowstorm!

MATERIALS
- ☐ One cup of water
- ☐ One tablespoon white paint
- ☐ Mixing bowl
- ☐ One glass jar with lid
- ☐ Baby oil
- ☐ Glitter
- ☐ Blue food coloring
- ☐ One fizzing tablet, such as Alka Seltzer

It is a good idea to gather your materials before you begin.

⋯The glitter looks like snow blowing!

STEPS

1. Mix the water and white paint in a bowl.

2. Fill the jar with baby oil until it is $3/4$ full.

3. Add food coloring and glitter to the oil.

4. Pour the paint and water mixture over the oil layer.

5. Drop the fizzing tablet in the jar.

6. The oil will remain at the top of the jar. The tablet pushes upward. The oil pushes the tablet back down. A snowstorm begins!

Snow can fall quickly during snowstorms and cover roads and sidewalks.

CHAPTER 2

What Causes a Snowstorm?

Snow is a form of **precipitation**. Rain is another form. The **atmosphere** between the clouds and the Earth is sometimes above 32 degrees Fahrenheit (0 degrees Celsius). That is the freezing point of water. Water droplets in the clouds do not freeze. This causes rainfall. The droplets freeze when the temperature is at or below freezing. The frozen droplets fall as snow.

Snow falls from the sky when it is too cold to rain.

A condition called a **front** forms when cold and warm air masses meet in the atmosphere. Cold air has a higher **density** than warm air. The gases in the atmosphere are packed closer together.

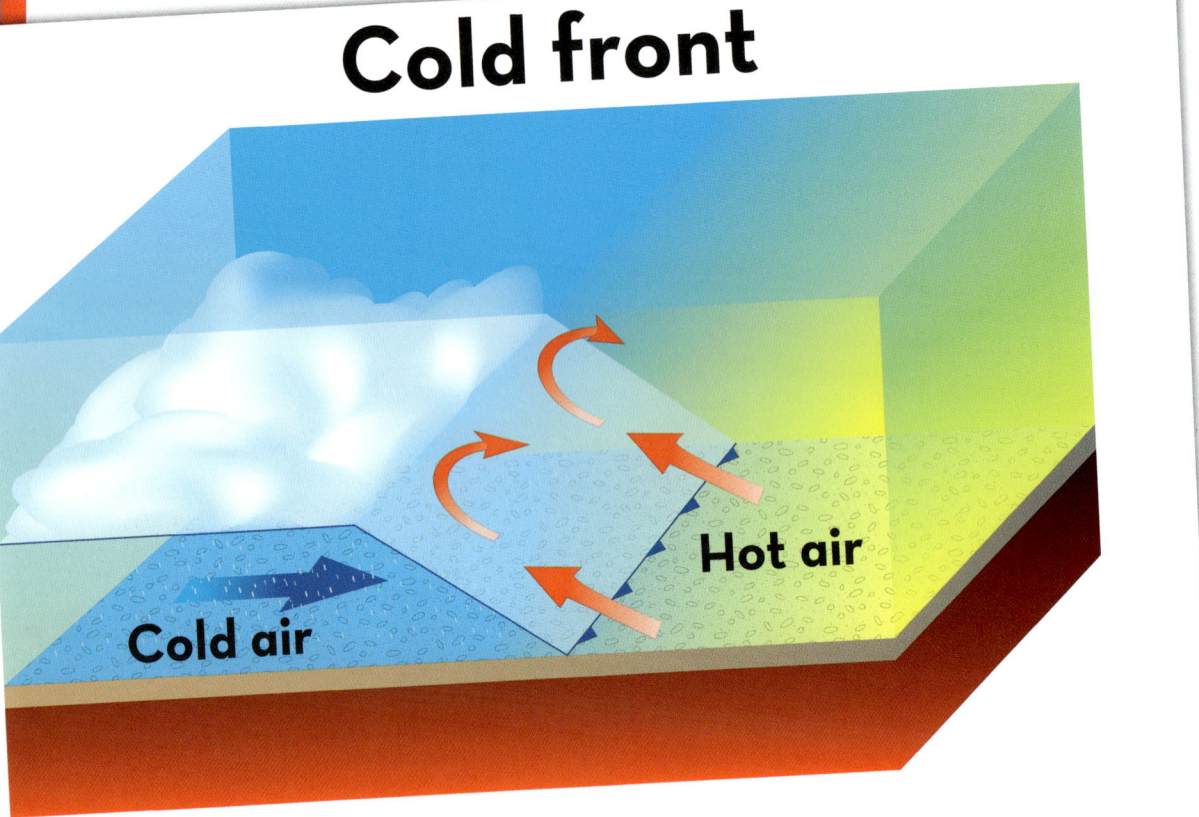

A cold front forms when warm air is pushed above cold air.

The warm air is less dense. It is pushed above the colder air. Warm air brings **water vapor** with it. The warm air collects the water vapor when it passes over water.

The vapor freezes when temperatures are cold enough. The small ice crystals in the clouds stick together. They become snowflakes. They get heavy enough to fall to the ground. Large amounts of snow become snowstorms. In the experiment, the paint and glitter look like falling snow.

DID YOU KNOW?

Snow can be wet or dry. Snowflakes that fall through cool, dry air are powdery. Snowflakes melt a little when the temperature is just above freezing. They become wet.

CHAPTER 3

What Kinds of Snowstorms Are There?

There are many kinds of snowstorms. Snow flurries are light snow showers. They fall for short periods of time. Very little snow piles up.

Snow squalls are short, strong snow showers. Heavy winds blow. The blowing snow makes it hard to see. Snow piles up very quickly.

Blowing snow can make it very hard to see.

Blizzards are the most powerful snowstorms. They produce heavy snowfall. Winds blow faster than 35 miles (56 km) per hour. It becomes hard to see. Blizzards can be dangerous. Heavy snow makes driving difficult. The cold can cause **hypothermia**, which means a person's body is too cold. Electricity may go out when heavy winds blow.

DID YOU KNOW?

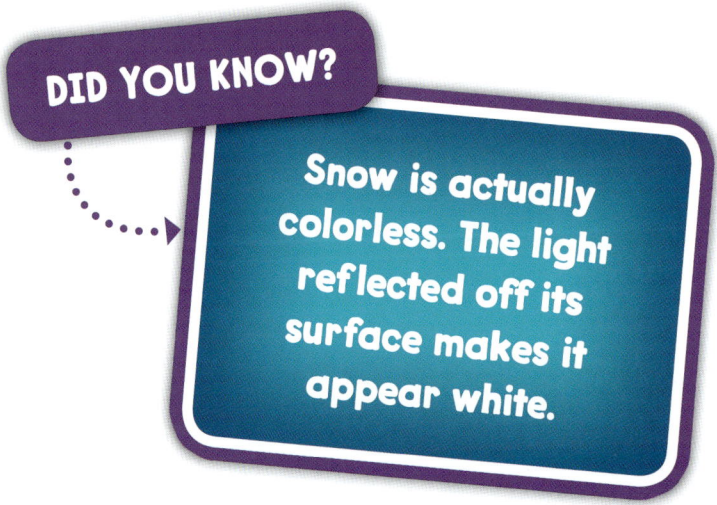

Snow is actually colorless. The light reflected off its surface makes it appear white.

It is important to bundle up to keep safe during a blizzard.

Always stay safe during a snowstorm. Dress warmly and cover all skin. Try not to go outside. Follow emergency directions in your town.

CHAPTER 4

Where Do Snowstorms Happen?

Snowstorms occur in many parts of the world. Greenland and parts of Europe experience snowstorms. The Siberian Peninsula has long, harsh winters. Snow may remain on the ground for more than half a year.

Siberia is famous for its harsh, snowy winters.

Blizzards and other snowstorms often leave a lot of snow behind.

Blizzards are common in Canada and Russia. The Great Plains region in the United States experiences blizzards. The Northeast region also has Nor'easters, or severe storms with heavy rain, snow, and wind.

DID YOU KNOW?

It does not snow very often in Antarctica, even though it is the coldest place on Earth. Constant cold temperatures prevent snow from melting when it does fall. It builds up over the years as ice sheets.

Mountains also get snowfall. The peaks are at a higher **altitude** than the land around them. Higher altitudes are colder. The atmosphere is thinner. Heat is lost as particles in the air move farther apart. Water vapor cools and freezes. Snow can be found all year long on some mountains.

Many mountains have snow on the ground in late spring. Others have snow that lasts year round.

Glossary

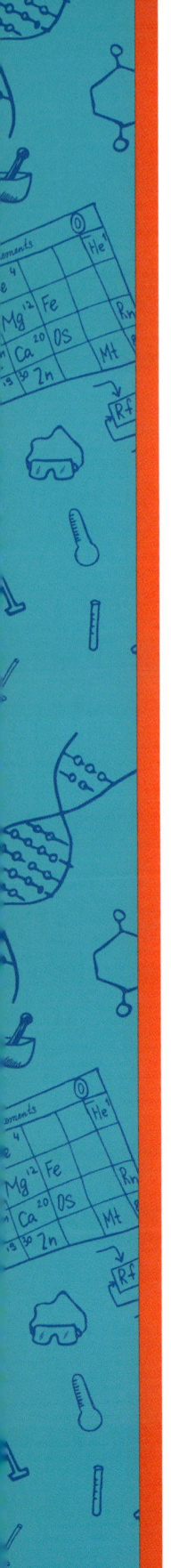

altitude (AL-ti-tood) Altitude is the height of anything above earth or sea level. Mountain peaks are at a very high altitude.

atmosphere (AT-mos-feer) The atmosphere is made of the gases surrounding the earth and is often called air. Snow falls down from clouds in the atmosphere.

density (DENS-i-tee) Density is the measurement of how close particles are in an object. Warm air has a lower density than cold air.

front (FRUNT) A front is the place in the atmosphere where cold and warm air masses meet. When warm air rises above cold air, a front is created.

hypothermia (hy-po-THER-me-uh) Hypothermia is when the body's temperature gets too cold. Hypothermia happens when people spend too long in the cold without warm clothes.

precipitation (pre-sip-i-TAY-shun) Precipitation is water falling in the form of rain, snow, hail, or sleet. Snow is a common form of precipitation in the winter.

water vapor (WAH-ter VAY-pur) Water vapor is water in the form of gas. When water vapor adds moisture to the air, snowflakes may form.

To Learn More

In the Library

Coss, Lauren. *Weird-but-True Facts about Weather.* Mankato, MN: The Child's World, 2013.

Jensen, Belinda. *A Snowstorm Shows Off: Blizzards.* Minneapolis, MN: Millbrook Press, 2016.

Zoehfeld, Kathleen Weidner. *What Makes a Blizzard?* New York, NY: HarperCollins, 2018.

On the Web

Visit our website for links about snowstorms:
childsworld.com/links

Note to Parents, Teachers, and Librarians: We routinely verify our Web links to make sure they are safe and active sites. So encourage your readers to check them out!

Index

altitude, 20
atmosphere, 8-9, 20

blizzards, 14, 19

density, 9-10

front, 9

hypothermia, 14

mountains, 20

Nor'easters, 19

precipitation, 8

snow flurries, 12
snow squalls, 12

water vapor, 10-11, 20